The
LITTLE BOOK OF
FLIRTING

D1344164

THE LITTLE BOOK OF FLIRTING

Summersdale Publishers Ltd
46 West Street
Chichester
West Sussex
PO19 1RP
UK

www.summersdale.com

Printed and bound in Malta

ISBN: 978-1-84953-906-7

Substantial discounts on bulk quantities of Summersdale books are available to corporations, professional associations and other organisations. For details contact general enquiries: telephone: +44 (0) 1243 771107, fax: +44 (0) 1243 786300 or email: enquiries@summersdale.com.

The —
LITTLE BOOK OF
FLIRTING

Sadie Cayman

Contents

INTRODUCTION

So you've decided you'd like to develop your skills as a flirt: someone who is radiant with beauty, intelligence and wit, attracting anybody they set their sights on. Congratulations!

First things first. In order to become an accomplished flirt, you'll need buckets of self-confidence. And here's a secret – even if you don't believe you have this naturally, faked confidence is just as good! All it takes is a moment's pep talk: look at yourself in the mirror and tell yourself, 'I am an attractive, interesting and funny person.' (But maybe not in public or if you have company.)

Once you've got your self-esteem soaring, you'll need a thorough knowledge of body language, some charming conversation openers, and some top tips on where and how to meet other attractive young things like you. Luckily, this book contains all you need.

Whether you treat your flirting as a complicated science or as a fun way to meet new people, this book will arm you with the skills and know-how to charm the pants off anyone. It'll help you get noticed, initiate and hold a stimulating conversation, give out the right signals and, most of all, become a world-class flirt.

MYSTERIES OF ATTRACTION COULD NOT ALWAYS BE EXPLAINED THROUGH LOGIC.

LISA KLEYPAS

THE BASICS

Before we delve into the exhilarating world of hook-ups, internet dating and real-life dates, let's take a quick tour of the marvels of the human body, and how we use it to create those small moments of electricity with the objects of our desires – these are the 'sparks' that people speak of.

Signs They're Single

Before you start putting your flirting into action, it's a good idea to work out (as far as possible without getting into stalker territory) whether the person you're interested in is single. Making sure they're available and seem interested before you make a move will save time and embarrassment for everyone involved.

Signs that someone is single and approachable:

✔ If they are playing with their hair, or glass, or touching their mouth, they may be feeling flirty.

✔ If their feet are pointing towards you it can be a subconscious way of displaying interest (but don't take this as a dead cert!).

✔ If they blush, pout or pucker their mouth, or lean towards you when you smile at them, they could be interested.

✔ If a group of friends are standing together, and one person (or more!) has wandering eyes, they are likely to be looking to meet someone.

✔ If one person breaks away from a group to head to the bathroom or bar alone, they could be on the prowl – making themselves more approachable.

Signs that someone is uninterested in your flirtatious advances:

✘ If someone is sitting with a group of friends, laughing or talking intently without glancing up from their partners, they are probably uninterested in being approached.

✘ If they're avoiding eye contact with you, that's a clear sign to leave them alone.

✘ If they're looking at their watch or phone, it's usually a sign that they're waiting for someone or are alone but don't want to be disturbed.

✘ Sagging shoulders, tapping feet and any sign of leaning away from you are all indications that they're not interested.

UNFORTUNATELY, EVEN IF YOUR
MARK IS WILLING TO FLIRT, YOU
CAN'T ASSUME THAT THEY ARE
INTERESTED AND AVAILABLE. WHILE
AROUND 30 PER CENT OF US FLIRT
WITH A RELATIONSHIP AS OUR END
GOAL, 25 PER CENT DO IT SIMPLY
FOR FUN. BUT A GOOD FLIRT CAN BE
ENJOYABLE EVEN IF IT DOESN'T
GO ANYWHERE, SO DON'T
BE DISHEARTENED!

Flirting Signals

As a species, we've built up such a number of non-verbal ways to say 'I fancy the pants off you' that conversation is barely necessary. These flirting signals have been tried and tested over generations, and, though they may seem clichéd, flirting appears to be one area where people are happy to accept convention.

The best thing about these signals is that, in most cases, if your crush doesn't respond in the desired way, you can brush a gesture off as a tic, or pretend you thought your foot was just caressing the table leg. And, if you're on the lookout for a potential mate, then someone who is displaying any or all of these signals (preferably aimed in your direction, not at the hot guy/girl on the next table) is probably a good person to approach.

BODY LANGUAGE

You may have heard the claim that up to 90 per cent
of first impressions are dictated by body language.
While the exact figure and the science behind it varies
from study to study, the basic fact is true – we really are
physical animals, and humans are incredibly adept at
decoding the subtle (and sometimes subconscious) social
cues given out by our gestures and posture.

For instance, a man is more likely to approach a woman
with uncrossed arms – folding them is generally seen to
be a position of defence, indicating either discomfort,
lack of trust, lack of interest or hostility. Slouching can be
a major turn-off, so if you want to be flawlessly attractive,
make sure you're sitting up straight! Leaning slightly
towards your conversational partner can also indicate
interest – as long as you're not staring them straight in
the eye at a millimetre's distance, of course. That's not a
good flirting technique for anybody.

THE MAJORITY OF WOMEN FIND
PERSONALITY AND LOOKS MUCH
MORE ATTRACTIVE THAN THE
AMOUNT OF MONEY A MAN HAS.
GOOD NEWS FOR BROKE FOLK!

HAIROGRAPHY

The hair toss is a flirty girl's Samwise Gamgee – always there when needed and unfailingly dependable in a crisis. You've seen it countless times: a beautiful lady in a bar flicks her hair back over one shoulder, triggering an avalanche of mesmerised men.

You needn't be dramatic about it, but a small gesture with your hair (tucking it behind your ear or twirling it in your fingers, for example) indicates that you're interested. Importantly, it also gives the object of your affections a subtle glimpse of your elegant (and usually covered-up) neck – which experts say is bound to create an instant sense of intimacy between the two of you.

FEELING FLIRTY

Touching someone you don't know very well is risky business: too much enthusiasm and you might poke an eye out. But played right, a light graze of your hand over theirs or a delicate brush over their forearm or thigh will get sparks flying. The forearm especially is packed with pleasure nerves which send signals to the limbic system – an area of the brain associated with trust and affection. This one really does depend on context, though – if you're not already sitting in a position conducive to such gestures, it's most definitely *not* advisable to stride up to someone and stroke their leg. Subtlety and lightness of touch are key.

Footsie is the podiatric equivalent of the arm graze, and is much easier to cover up as an accident if the response is, 'Why the hell are you playing with my foot?'

IF YOU DON'T FLIRT, YOU'RE PROBABLY DEAD INSIDE.

KATHARINE TOWNE

MIMICKING

If you've ever been in conversation with a good friend and noticed that the two of you are sitting in exactly the same position, then you're already aware of how this one works. It's usually a subconscious act to mimic or mirror the body language of someone we admire, but it can be very effective when used consciously. If you spot that the person you're interested in is mirroring your chin-in-hand or casual arm-over-the-back-of-the-chair position, then odds are that you're in.

THE EYES HAVE IT

Holding eye contact is a sure-fire way to create an electric connection. Even if two people are complete strangers, it has been proven that maintaining intense eye contact for two minutes can create strong feelings of passion akin to love. There's real science behind it; when we look someone in the eyes our bodies produce a chemical called phenylethylamine, and it's this that makes us feel like we're in love – so don't knock it till you've tried it.

In real-life situations, however, two minutes of unbroken eye contact is rarely achievable or desirable. When it comes to casual flirting a second or two longer than usual is sufficient. Eye-contact tolerance levels may vary slightly from person to person, but studies show that a non-romantic glance lasts up to 1.2 seconds, whereas a sultry gaze is anything up to 3 seconds. Longer than that and the object of your desire is likely to start feeling rather uncomfortable.

STUDIES HAVE SHOWN THAT WE'RE
A NATURALLY UNASSUMING BUNCH
— IT TAKES, ON AVERAGE, THREE
GLANCES AT SOMEONE BEFORE THEY
WILL REGISTER YOUR INTEREST.
JUST MAKE SURE YOU REMEMBER TO
LOOK AWAY EVERY ONCE IN A WHILE!

FACIAL EXPRESSIONS

A warm, genuine smile is sometimes all it takes to start up a flirty conversation. But how to tell the genuine article from a well-crafted imitation? If the eyes are unaffected – if they remain fully open, or if you don't see crow's feet appear at the outer edges of the eyes – the smile is probably false. Similarly, if you can see a person's bottom teeth (like when you're saying 'cheeeese' for the camera), they're probably giving you a fake smile. Feelings of affection can't be forced and neither can a smile – it seems natural, then, that a genuine smile is an indicator of mutual attraction and liking. Coy smiles, happy smiles and guffaws of laughter at that hilarious joke you made all get a big tick on the flirting checklist.

OF ALL THE THINGS YOU
WEAR, YOUR EXPRESSION
IS THE MOST IMPORTANT.

JANET LANE

VOICE

Even when we focus on the way you speak, it's *still* not only about the words you use. This isn't to say you can blather on about anything, but there are more nuances to the art of conversation than many people realise.

For men, a deep voice is indicative of high levels of testosterone, so by the very workings of human nature women are programmed to find a low, steady voice attractive. In this situation, a woman's voice would tend to be higher than usual, as the pitch rises when they're attracted to somebody.

Letting your voice ebb and flow, changing in tone and pace, can also arouse interest – yes, really! For example, if you start off with a quickstep of words and then switch into a slower, lilting voice, that switch will provoke the listener into being more interested in what you have to say. This works with volume, too, but we don't recommend extremes of whispering and yelling – let's keep it subtle, people.

CONVERSATION

Striking up a conversation with a stranger: one of life's biggest challenges. For a good flirt, the ideal conversation should be at the '*medium talk*' level. Sure, you can start off with small talk and work your way up, but it's always best to avoid the heavier topics, such as politics or religion. The trick to making conversations flow is getting your partner talking about themselves, or something they love.

Open questions are great for finding out what they're interested in – e.g. 'What are your hobbies?' Once they've started to open up, be sure to keep the conversation flowing – asking how they got into a specific hobby, for instance. These details often get overlooked, so your conversation partner will appreciate being given the opportunity to just talk. If you find a point of interest, then bingo! You win a gold 'successful conversation' star. But, of course, if you find yourself mind-numbingly bored by what they have to say, you can always make your excuses and leave, and take it as a narrow escape.

The most important part of any conversation is *listening*. It's increasingly rare to find someone who is committed wholeheartedly to a conversation, and not staring at their phone or looking for someone better to talk to. By giving someone your whole attention, you will make them feel special, encouraging those butterflies that'll lead to them being attracted to you.

Humour is a great ice-breaker, but make sure you keep it natural. Unless you're a professional comedian (and by that I mean you actually do it for a living, not 'I wrote a comic once'), cracking joke after joke in place of normal conversation soon gets tiring. But a sense of humour and the occasional funny comment will go down well. Just make sure your humour isn't too rude or swear-filled, at least until you get to know each other well enough to take it to the sexy-joke level.

ONE CANNOT BE ALWAYS LAUGHING AT A MAN WITHOUT NOW AND THEN STUMBLING ON SOMETHING WITTY.

JANE AUSTEN

Teasing is one of flirting's strongest techniques. The traditional tease will take the form of affectionate ribbing about something you know the other person doesn't take too seriously (for instance, you wouldn't insult someone's appearance or a personality trait that they were insecure about), and is usually followed by nudging, and a giggly, insincere 'Stop it!' As long as you've established a rapport, good-humoured teasing is one of the most effective ways to ensure a connection.

A word about **compliments**. If you're going to tackle this beast, there are four golden rules:

- Be sincere. Anything less than sincerity will make you look like a sarcastic arsehole.

- Don't go over the top. Nobody wants a drooling admirer.

- Don't be too blunt. 'You've got a great rack' will be too direct in at least 99 per cent of all flirting situations.

- Avoid compliments on physical appearance. Instead, focus on an item of clothing, or an attribute such as their personality or dancing style. There is one exception to this rule, however: most people don't mind being told they have beautiful eyes.

SEX APPEAL IS FIFTY PER CENT WHAT YOU'VE GOT AND FIFTY PER CENT WHAT PEOPLE THINK YOU'VE GOT.

SOPHIA LOREN

VARIOUS OUTDATED LAWS IN
NEW YORK CITY SEEM TO WANT TO
KILL OUR FUN. ONE STATES THAT
FLIRTING IS PUNISHABLE BY A $25
FINE WHICH COULD BE DEALT OUT
SIMPLY FOR LOOKING AT SOMEONE
'SUGGESTIVELY'. IT IS TECHNICALLY
STILL EVEN ILLEGAL FOR WOMEN TO
WEAR 'BODY-HUGGING' CLOTHING!

In a Nutshell:
Top Flirting Tips

☺ **Exude confidence** in your body language and conversation, and **relax**. Speak slowly and calmly, and don't allow yourself to panic. Remember, they're only people – if the worst happens (say you spit in their face while talking, or spill your drink down their outfit) retain your poise and simply remove yourself from the situation... and the bar. And possibly the town. And you can always change your name.

☺ **Find out what's holding you back**, and address it. If you're feeling insecure about your appearance, perhaps now's the time to seize the day and get that fancy haircut that'll make you feel irresistible, or to hit the gym for a shot of endorphins and a boost of morale. If you're insecure about interacting with new people, start small – ask a shop assistant how their day's been, or start a conversation with a colleague you don't usually speak to. Practice makes perfect!

🙂 Set yourself **flirting challenges**. If you're not naturally confident, taking flirting as a game can help you lighten up and enjoy yourself more, which in turn will make you appear more attractive to others, so it's a win-win situation. These could be small ('I will talk to at least one new person today'), adventurous ('I will use three different chat-up lines tonight') or outrageous ('I will invite someone on an insta-date today' – an insta-date being a spontaneous date where you drop everything and go, right there, right then).

🙂 **Emulate someone you admire.** We all know that one person who seems to effortlessly chat to strangers and is always surrounded by hot admirers. Study what they do that makes them so interesting – how do they present themselves? What do they emphasise about themselves? Watch them (discreetly, of course) and have a go at replicating it yourself.

☺ **Go somewhere new**, where no one knows you. You'll feel less self-conscious about putting all these tricks into action, and you can create a whole new, confident, flirtatious persona.

☺ Once you know your flirting partner's **name**, use it several times throughout your conversation. It shows attentiveness, makes it clear that you're interested in getting to know them, and will make them feel special. However, if you're not confident that you can do this without it sounding odd, maybe give this one a miss.

☺ Keep **chewing gum** or mints in your pocket/ bag. Fresh breath is sexy, people. Plus, being able to offer one to somebody is one of the easiest conversation openers out there.

☺ Being a **good listener** is often cited as one of the most attractive qualities a person can have, and it's essential to creating a good rapport, so **pay**

attention to what your date is saying. Make an effort to repeat back snippets of the conversation (not word for word) and to talk about the things they're interested in. This helps to communicate that you care about what they have to say, which will make them feel good about themselves – and when they feel good, they'll feel good about you, too.

Make the other person feel special. Give them your undivided attention, listen to them, and pay them genuine, specific compliments (nothing generic or clichéd, please). Using the word 'we' can also help create a sense of intimacy between you, so try dropping it into conversation a few times.

Be positive! Nobody likes a whiner, and in dating it's especially important. Negativity has consistently been ranked as a top turn-off for first meetings, so try to refrain from telling that story about how terrible your job is, or from whingeing about how long you had to wait at the bar.

☺ **Leave them wanting more.** This is an important one! If you're having the time of your life and you get positive signals from the other person that they're enjoying your company too, then by all means stay up chatting all night. It could be the basis of a strong relationship. However, if you want to keep the situation light-hearted and your options open, leaving them wanting more is a good policy to follow. End the conversation at a natural point rather than letting it fizzle out awkwardly, so that you leave them with a sparkling impression of you and a warm glow after your first meeting. The next time you meet them you'll both be eager to pick up where you left off.

YOU HAVE ONE CHANCE TO MAKE A FIRST IMPRESSION.

KEVIN McCARTHY

A STUDY FROM MANCHESTER UNIVERSITY BACKED UP THE LONG-HELD PIECE OF WISDOM THAT RED LIPS ON WOMEN ARE THE MOST ATTRACTIVE TO THE OPPOSITE SEX. TRACKING THE EYE MOVEMENTS OF MEN SHOWED THAT THEY LOOKED AT PINK LIPS FOR 6.7 SECONDS ON AVERAGE, BUT RED LIPS HELD THEIR GAZE AN IMPRESSIVE 7.3 SECONDS.

WHAT NOT TO DO

If you're tempted to use any of the following as part of your flirting repertoire, here is some sound advice: *Don't do it.*

✘ Wolf whistling

✘ Bum pinching

✘ Winking

✘ 'Do you come here often?'

PEOPLE ARE EITHER CHARMING OR TEDIOUS.

OSCAR WILDE

Seven Schools of Flirting

Compliment-athon

Everyone enjoys a compliment, but it's way easier to take the mickey out of each other than actually admit you might like one another. Getting someone's number through sheer flattery should only be attempted by serious smooth-talkers.

Laugh a Minute

They say humour is the highest form of intelligence, and perhaps, if you make the other person laugh long enough, they'll accept the invitation back to yours just to use your bathroom. Just make sure your jokes are actually funny and that the other person isn't staring at you stonily before you launch your barrage of hilarity at them.

Overly Sexual

This can either be the most embarrassing approach, or the hottest. If you fancy the pants off each other, whispered dirty words can be a big turn-on – just make sure you're certain that they weren't making eyes at somebody else. You'll need a thick skin if you're going to put this high-risk tactic into action!

Cheesy

Use lines like 'That dress looks great on you. It'd look even better on my bedroom floor' OR 'They say everything's made in China these days. It's good to see some things are still made in heaven'... and you're set! Even if your line falls flat on its face, at least you'll get a laugh (whether it's 'with you' or 'at you' remains to be seen).

Au Naturel

Sometimes, all it takes is a 'hey'. Smile, show your interest, and start a natural conversation where you're just being yourself, rather than putting on any moves. Although not dramatic, this works wonders with the right person.

Physical Flirter

Meeting the person of your dreams in a sweaty bar and having them push up against you might be steamy. Having a stranger rub themselves on your leg uninvited may constitute sexual harassment. It's a fine line.

Drunk Flirting

'I think youajr'eaje really hawttt.' The effectiveness of this technique usually depends on how drunk the person you're flirting with is.

THIS IS ONE FOR THE MEN: CHEWING
A STICK OF CELERY RELEASES
ANDROSTENONE AND ANDROSTENOL
ODOUR MOLECULES INTO YOUR MOUTH.
THESE PHEROMONES BOOST YOUR
AROUSAL AND, IN TURN, TRIGGER
YOUR BODY TO SEND OUT SCENTS
THAT MAKE YOU MORE DESIRABLE
TO WOMEN.

LEAD ME NOT INTO TEMPTATION; I CAN FIND THE WAY MYSELF.

RITA MAE BROWN

Part One:

THE HOOK-UP

Where to Meet People

So, you're armed with the basic knowledge for a
successful flirt. Now you need to find someone to
practise on. If you're single and ready to mingle, read on.
If you already have someone in mind as the target
of your flirting skills, you can move swiftly on to
the next section.

AT A BAR

Pubs and bars are the most obvious place to 'pick someone up', and with reason. They're understood to be public zones where it's socially acceptable to talk to strangers. Plus, there's alcohol involved. However, there are still some restrictions. For example, if someone is sitting in a back corner, furthest away from the counter, they probably want to be left alone. Hanging around by the bar or at the tables closest to it, on the other hand, is often a signal that a person is open to meeting somebody new.

The Moves

If you want to be seen as approachable at a bar, it's best to be with more than one friend. Having two other wing-buddies will help you appear more approachable and, if you hit it off with someone, your companion won't feel abandoned or ignored.

Talking to the bartender or other customers at the bar also gives off the impression that you're friendly and approachable, and starting an open, non-flirtatious conversation with a stranger makes it easier for someone else – hopefully a smoking hottie – to join in.

Conversation Starters

The common ground: What's the betting that drunk guy's going to be on the floor within ten minutes?

The context: Oof, you're on the flaming tequila shots already?! Big night ahead then...

The opinion opener: Hey, are you local? Some friends and I are looking for somewhere to go after here – where would you recommend?

The cheesy: You're hotter than the bottom of my laptop after demolishing an entire series on Netflix.

THE PROBLEM WITH HUMAN ATTRACTION IS NOT KNOWING IF IT WILL BE RETURNED.

BECCA FITZPATRICK

AT A PARTY

Spotting a potential love interest at a party is great – the chances are you already have some mutual friends, and some things in common to discuss. The conversation starters are limitless and, compared to a bar, a party is a far more casual environment in which to start a conversation with a stranger. Plus, you're probably all stuck together in one place for the duration of the night, so you don't need to panic that your target is going to disappear. In short: it's the perfect place to act cool, break the ice with some easy conversation, and enjoy yourself!

The Moves

One of the best ways to create an immediate sense of fun and intimacy is to perform a task and invite someone else to do it with you. Perhaps you've offered to help refill the snacks and you need a hand, or you'd like their help creating a 'surprise' for the guest of honour. Or you could see if they want to play a (two-player) card game or drinking game, to break any monotony. By doing something together, you make the other person feel special and break the ice, so there's no need for awkward conversation – it's a win–win situation.

Alternatively, parties are the perfect place to play the 'don't I know you?' card. You can adapt it however you like – perhaps you start chatting to someone about something obscure, before 'realising' that they're not who you thought they were. Depending on how cheesy you feel, you could say 'Oops, I thought you were someone else, sorry. But you're a *lot* cuter.'

Conversation Starters

The goofy: 'accidentally' bump into them and say: Oh sorry, I become a total klutz around cute girls/guys.

The opinion opener: I'm meant to be at home doing some research on XX – could you help me out? What's your opinion of XX?

The dare: I dare you to refill the punch bowl with straight vodka and see how long it takes anyone to notice.

The quest: There's gotta be some food around here somewhere. Wanna help me find some?

A SURVEY BY *GLAMOUR*
MAGAZINE SHOWED THAT 75
PER CENT OF WOMEN HAVE
FANTASISED ABOUT MEN
IN A FIREMAN'S UNIFORM.
PROBABLY ONLY A GOOD
PICK-UP TECHNIQUE IF
YOU'RE INTENDING TO GO TO
A FANCY-DRESS PARTY, OR
YOU'RE ON YOUR WAY HOME
FROM THE FIRE STATION, THOUGH.

IT IS ONLY SHALLOW
PEOPLE WHO DO NOT
JUDGE BY APPEARANCES.

OSCAR WILDE

SPORTS
EVENTS

There's nothing more appealing than finding out that someone you know is already into one of your biggest interests. Whatever your sport of choice, the fact that they're there too gives you immediate common ground to start from, and endless opportunities for conversation based on the goings-on of the game. Unless you're watching a chess match, there's likely to be lots of action to keep you interested (and prevent any awkward silences) and enough time for you to have a chilled-out conversation and not have to rush. Add to that the fact that you can probably hear each other speak and don't have to yell over dodgy music, and sports events may just be the greatest place to find a hook-up ever invented.

The Moves

It's the perfect environment: simply ask their opinion of a certain player, or who they think is going to win. It sets you up for an animated conversation with lots of spaces to drop a teasing, flirty comment. Once you've got the ball rolling it's time to step up the flirting game by implementing all the techniques we talked about earlier, and letting your personality shine. You can also move on from the regular questions to the more playful ones ('I bet you two drinks that there'll be a foul in the next two minutes'; 'How are you celebrating after our team wins?') or tell them that charming story about how you got that sporting scar in primary school...

There's one danger at sporting events: people often attend without their partners, so a person on their own isn't necessarily single. While it doesn't matter if you make a total tit out of yourself (you'll probably never see them again), it might be uncomfortable to sit next to each for 90 minutes after a total chat-up fail.

Conversation Starters

The opinion opener: I can't believe XX won Player of the Match last time. Do you think he deserved it?

The challenge: You think you know your sports? I bet you can't tell me (insert related question here)!

The cheesy: I bet you play football, because you're a keeper.

The cheesy number 2: I wish you were wearing a team shirt. That way I wouldn't have to ask for your name and number.

HERE'S A QUICK FACT FROM SPEED DATING. MOST PEOPLE MAKE A DECISION ABOUT THEIR ATTRACTION TO A PARTNER WITHIN 3 SECONDS.

More Meeting Places

Work: It's commonplace for a reason – seeing and possibly interacting with someone day in, day out, is bound to result in a certain amount of interest and liking. Four out of ten workplace relationships result in marriage, which proves that it can truly be the basis of a strong relationship. On the other hand, the workplace relationships that crash and burn often result in public humiliation, hugely embarrassing work situations and one of you having to find a new job.

Through friends and family: According to some research, you're twice as likely to find a date through mutual acquaintances than at the bar.

Coffee shops, cafes, shopping centres: Striking up a conversation with someone eating lunch or having a coffee alone can be a successful tactic – just make sure they are giving out signs that they're happy to be approached.

College/evening classes: You already share a mutual interest – romance is just around the corner! Bonus sexy points if you meet at a dance class or foreign language course.

Wine tasting: Alcohol and easy conversational topics abound.

Art gallery: You don't need to know anything about art to strike up a conversation about a piece you find interesting. What do you think the piece means? What stands out to you? And what are all those squiggly bits about? A gallery is also seen as being both unusual and romantic.

Dog walking: Dogs are wonderful for 'accidentally' tying you and your future beau up in a tangled lead.

Where not to meet people: Though they can be great for dates, restaurants or cinemas aren't generally conducive to spontaneous conversation, or to introducing yourself to strangers.

FOR ME IT'S ALWAYS ABOUT FIRST IMPRESSIONS. I TRUST MY INSTINCTS.

BILLY ZANE

The Next Move

So, you've been chatting to a hot guy or gal all night, and things are going well. You've shown off your charm, style, humour and outstanding personality to their best effect. Now what? Well, you have several options:

If you feel the time is right, move in for **the kiss**. Signs that the other person is ready for a kiss are glances at your mouth, physical closeness, their head tilting slightly to one side and parted lips. If these signs are all on display, then there's a good chance your kiss will be reciprocated.

If you're feeling mischievous, moving in for a kiss but then turning your head to peck them on the cheek instead at the last minute will drive them crazy and make them eager to see you again.

If you're not ready to go in for a kiss but want to see them again, make sure to **ask for their number.** You don't want all your hard work to go to waste by missing the opportunity to stay in contact. If they say no, no harm done - at least if you've asked, you won't be moping around over the one that got away.

If things are going swimmingly, perhaps you're ready to - *oooh* - **invite them back to your place.** Don't rush into anything you're uncomfortable with, but go with the flow if it feels natural. Just remember to be safe, and have fun.

Remember, **don't force things.** Even if you feel you've received all the right signals, if at the end of the night they don't want to go any further, that's their prerogative. It's far better to go home nursing a little hurt pride than to make yourself look like an arse by being too pushy. Remember: anything that isn't an unambiguous YES is actually a NO.

I THINK THE EYES FLIRT
MOST. THERE ARE SO
MANY WAYS TO USE THEM.

ANNA HELD

**THE AVERAGE PERSON SPENDS
OVER 20,000 MINUTES OF THEIR
LIVES KISSING. THAT'S AROUND
TWO WEEKS.**

Part Two:
TECHNOLOGY

Ah, technology. We're so advanced these days that we'll soon have no need for light arm grazes and hair flicking, as they'll have been replaced by emojis and swipes. But, as with all new developments, although there are good points, there are also the potential pitfalls that end with us sending a message to someone on Tinder telling them our most intimate fantasies and then asking if they like sausage rolls.

Online Dating

Tinder, Happn, Match.com and Plenty of Fish are old
hat now, but it's worth repeating some essentials of
netiquette here.

Don't:

✘ Use photos of other people (you'll get found out)

✘ Lie about your character and interests

✘ Disclose details you wouldn't want strangers knowing

✘ Insult others

✘ Believe everything other people write about themselves

✘ Arrange to meet people you don't know in private

Do:

✔ Use recent photos of yourself

✔ Write about your interests (if they're interesting!)

✔ Be yourself

✔ Flirt with people who have the same interests

✔ Have fun, but be wary of who you are talking to

✔ Keep the tone light-hearted

SEDUCTION IS ALWAYS MORE SINGULAR AND SUBLIME THAN SEX AND IT COMMANDS THE HIGHER PRICE.

JEAN BAUDRILLARD

OK on Social Media But Not OK in Real Life

Social media allows us the freedom to behave in ways that we wouldn't normally dream of in real-life flirting situations. Here are just some examples:

☺ Sending selfies will work on social media, but it's not quite the same if you get out a stack of photos that you just happened to have in your bag.

☺ Expressing your thoughts and feelings through emojis cannot work in real life – holding up flashcards just won't cut it.

☺ Poking someone is fine on Facebook but has completely different connotations in real life.

☺ Using LOL (although slightly annoying) is still better than literally laughing out loud for a minute. And as for PMSL: let's not even go there.

☺ A little bit of online stalking might be a good idea before a first date, but hiding out in the bushes and checking their every move is not only bad, it's illegal.

Digital Turn-offs

According to a survey, the biggest online flirting turn-offs are:

✗ Bad or informal spelling

✗ Lack of punctuation and grammar

✗ Multiple exclamation marks!!!!

✗ all lower case words. even after full stops

✗ Excessive slang (LOL, TBH, etc.)

✗ Sending messages at night – between 11 p.m. and 7 a.m. (Why are people doing this?! Beauty sleep is important.) Especially if it's a booty call when you haven't met yet.

But, perhaps defying expectation, a popular dating site's survey revealed that regular emoji users went on more dates than those who kept it strictly alphabetical.

IT HAS BEEN CLAIMED THAT BEING
ATTRACTED TO SOMEONE MAKES IT
HARDER TO LIE TO THEM, SO BE ON
YOUR GUARD NEXT TIME YOU'RE ON
A FLIRTING MISSION — YOU DON'T
WANT TO END UP BLURTING OUT
SECRETS SUCH AS 'I LIKE
YOUR FACE'.

SHE GAVE ME A SMILE
I COULD FEEL IN MY
HIP POCKET.

RAYMOND CHANDLER

Part Three:
THE DATES

So you've made the first move and invited someone out on a date. Congratulations! Now you've just got to make it through several hours alone together, and hope you don't mess up. Good luck with that...

First dates really can be nerve-wracking, but with a little help you can ensure you give yourself the greatest chance of avoiding a dating disaster.

Places to Go

Suggesting where to go on a date carries an enormous amount of pressure. If you suggest just going for a drink, your date might think you're not putting any thought into it.

Choosing an exciting or adrenaline-fuelled date, such as go-karting, could be a good option, as a psychological link has been found between danger and physical/romantic attraction. Unusual ideas show creativity, thought and effort – a dance class, for instance.

Choosing somewhere there are opportunities for physical contact will allow for quicker bonding, such as a festival, or hiking.

To boost your confidence, pick somewhere you'll feel comfortable. Most of all, think about your date – what would they find interesting and fun, and would give you the chance to get to know each other better? Have they mentioned something they've always wanted to do, or did you discuss a mutual interest that would create a great date?

A SURVEY FOUND THAT THE
WORST PLACES TO SUGGEST FOR
A FIRST DATE ARE FAST-FOOD
RESTAURANTS, YOUR CHILD'S
BIRTHDAY PARTY OR SCHOOL PLAY,
YOUR PARENTS' HOUSE, STRIP
CLUBS, X-RATED SCREENINGS AT
THE CINEMA, SWINGERS' PARTIES,
A PARTY WHERE YOUR EX WILL
BE, CHURCH ACTIVITIES OR
WINDOW SHOPPING.

First-date Etiquette

Do:

✔ Show up on time

✔ Relax and be confident

✔ Be honest about your feelings, but try not to appear too eager.

Don't:

✘ Talk about your ex partners

✘ Talk about yourself non-stop

✘ Flirt with other people around you

✘ Mention marriage, kids, politics or religion.

THE
DINNER DATE

So you've gone for the classic first-date setting. There's a reason it's such a popular choice – a restaurant is somewhere neutral, which provides you with something to do with your hands and something to comment on if the conversation falters (and there's often wine involved). You could impress your date even further by picking a restaurant with a quirky interior design, an unusual menu, or a stunning view – further elements with which to fuel your conversation.

The Moves

Get closer. Request a small table (preferably when you make the booking, not when you arrive!); if the waiter tries to direct you to a big, brightly lit and exposed table, ask for something a little more cosy. Sitting next to each other in a booth or side-by-side round the corner of a table (as opposed to the traditional date set-up facing each other) allows your bodies to touch and your arm to graze theirs, creating a feeling of intimacy. You can still look each other in the eyes, but the closer physical proximity will create more of a bond than if you're staring at each other across the gaping chasm of a table.

Be on your best behaviour! Tipping, being polite but assertive with the staff, and making sure your date is comfortable will only reflect well on you.

Finally, if the date's going well, don't order coffee in the restaurant. That way you get to invite your date back to yours for an entirely different type of dessert.

APPARENTLY WOMEN ARE
MORE ATTRACTED TO MEN
WEARING BLUE THAN ANY
OTHER COLOUR. THERE'S THAT
PULLING OUTFIT SORTED THEN.

MOVIE NIGHT

Taking your date to see a movie has been a stalwart of dating and flirtation for a century. The Drifters were singing about it way back in the sixties, so it's hardly innovative. But, if it ain't broke...

The Moves

Sure, it's cute to share popcorn, and there's always the chance of an accidental hand-brush as you both reach for it at the same time, but munching noises are a total turn-off. If you do go for snacks, eat them politely.

Get touchy-feely. Scary films are perfect for this – if one of you gets scared, the other can offer a protective arm. Gently touching your knees together creates a small moment of tension. The volume of the film also makes it hard to talk, so you'll just *have* to lean in close to make witty comments to each other.

But, whatever you do, don't get so distracted thinking about ways to turn the film into a flirtathon that you miss the film entirely. Your partner may actually want to watch it, so if you sense they're uncomfortable with your hilarious commentary you could restrict it to some low-level hand-holding. Plus, it's usually good conversation fodder to actually discuss the film afterwards, and you'll look like a buffoon if you haven't a clue what was going on.

I SUSPECT THE SECRET OF PERSONAL ATTRACTION IS LOCKED UP IN OUR UNIQUE IMPERFECTIONS, FLAWS AND FRAILTIES.

HUGH MACKAY

First-date Conversation Starters

The key to conversation starters is to make your date feel like they fit naturally into your conversation. Asking leading questions out of the blue can sometimes feel like an interview, and can put your date on edge.

Here's an example:

Instead of jumping in with, 'What's your greatest unrealised ambition?' (which sounds like you've plucked it out of a hat), try this:

'There are so many things I've always wanted to do but haven't got round to yet. You must find that, too? What's the biggest thing you'd love to achieve?'

Try adapting these questions into normal conversation:

- What do you value most in a friendship?

- What's your most treasured memory?

- What achievement are you most proud of?

- If you could ask for three wishes in life, what would they be?

- If you could find out the answer to one big question, what would it be?

- What's your most embarrassing moment?

- Tell me something I don't know about you.

- What do you find most attractive in other people?

And if you can't think of anything off the top of your head, you can always play the 'dub other people's conversations' game – as long as there is more than one other person in the room with you, it's the perfect way to fill a silence and make each other laugh with your ridiculous ideas.

LOVE WITHOUT CONVERSATION IS IMPOSSIBLE.

MORTIMER ADLER

FORTY-THREE PER CENT OF SINGLES
SAID THAT FRESH BREATH WAS THE
MOST IMPORTANT THING BEFORE
A FIRST DATE. WHERE'S THAT
CHEWING GUM?

Keeping the Flirting Flame Alive

Congratulations, you've successfully flirted your way through your first date! But the flirting doesn't end there. The secret to good relationships is that couples continue to have fun together, to stay light-hearted, and to enjoy each other's company, keeping the sense of excitement that probably characterised their first few meetings.

So, even if you've already been on 101 dates with your partner, why not flick back through this book and give some of the other ideas a go? After the thrill of getting to know each other has died down, it'll be a pleasant surprise to be treated like you're on a first date, or even to pretend you're chatting each other up for the first time all over again. Thinking up a romantic idea for a date night, or simply giving out subtle flirting gestures at a public event, can keep the excitement and anticipation levels high – and remember, you're never too old to flirt!

ON AVERAGE, THERE ARE NEARLY
200,000 PEOPLE HAVING SEX AT ANY
ONE TIME. NO PRESSURE, THEN.

ATTRACTION IS BEYOND OUR WILL OR IDEAS SOMETIMES.

JULIETTE BINOCHE

Staying Safe

You've heard these things before, but they cannot be repeated too many times. It is *essential* that you follow these rules when meeting someone for the first time, or if you're going out on your own:

- **Don't give away personal information** (at least for the first three dates)

- **Meet in a public place** – preferably somewhere busy and well-lit

- **Tell someone where you're going**, and when you expect to be back

- **Drink responsibly** – remember, flirting should be fun, not embarrassing

- **Listen to your instincts** – if something doesn't feel right, remove yourself from the situation as fast as you can

- **Have a back-out plan** – this is where the best friend just waiting with an 'emergency' really can come in useful. Alternatively, pre-arrange a taxi or lift home so that you must leave at a set point.

Good luck, and happy flirting!

If you're interested in finding out more about our books, find us on Facebook at **SUMMERSDALE PUBLISHERS** and follow us on Twitter at **@SUMMERSDALE**.

WWW.SUMMERSDALE.COM